A DAY IN THE LIFE OF A BUILDER

THIS EDITION

Produced for DK by WonderLab Group LLC
Jennifer Emmett, Erica Green, Kate Hale, *Founders*

Editor Maya Myers; **Photography Editor** Nicole DiMella; **Managing Editor** Rachel Houghton;
Designers Project Design Company; **Researcher** Michelle Harris; **Copy Editor** Lori Merritt;
Indexer Connie Binder; **Proofreader** Susan K. Hom; **Series Reading Specialist** Dr. Jennifer Albro

First American Edition, 2025
Published in the United States by DK Publishing, a division of Penguin Random House LLC
1745 Broadway, 20th Floor, New York, NY 10019

Copyright © 2025 Dorling Kindersley Limited
24 25 26 27 10 9 8 7 6 5 4 3 2 1
001-345390-March/2025

All rights reserved.
Without limiting the rights under the copyright reserved above, no part of this publication may be reproduced, stored in or introduced into a retrieval system, or transmitted, in any form, or by any means (electronic, mechanical, photocopying, recording, or otherwise), without the prior written permission of the copyright owner.
Published in Great Britain by Dorling Kindersley Limited

A catalog record for this book is available from the Library of Congress.
HC ISBN: 978-0-5939-6246-6
PB ISBN: 978-0-5939-6245-9

DK books are available at special discounts when purchased in bulk for sales promotions, premiums, fund-raising, or educational use. For details, contact:
DK Publishing Special Markets, 1745 Broadway, 20th Floor, New York, NY 10019
SpecialSales@dk.com

Printed and bound in China
Super Readers Lexile® levels 310L to 490L
Lexile® is the registered trademark of MetaMetrics, Inc. Copyright © 2024 MetaMetrics, Inc. All rights reserved.

The publisher would like to thank the following for their kind permission to reproduce their images:
a=above; c=center; b=below; l=left; r=right; t=top; b/g=background
123RF.com: Valery Voennyy / Vvoennyy 21t; **Depositphotos Inc:** Dusanpetkovic 13;
Dreamstime.com: Patrick Allen 14, 30cla, Leonid Andronov 7bc, Auremar 8, Dibrova 7bl, Oleg Dudko 22t, Hikrcn 1, Caeri Hiraman 6b, 30cl, Irochka 25bl, Issalina 25bc, Dmitry Kalinovsky 24, Philip Kinsey 15clb, Anne Kitzman 7cr, Peter Lewis 26b, Jim Parkin 10–11, Santos06 15c, Nipa Sawangsri 12, Sergiy1975 19b, 30bl, Sergey Spritnyuk 20, Edwin Verin 22-23, Steve Woods / Woodsy007 30clb; **Getty Images:** Brand X Pictures / Huntstock 26-27;
Getty Images / iStock: E+ / Alvarez 3, E+ / FatCamera 15t, E+ / Hispanolistic 21b, E+ / Kali9 10b, 16-17, E+ / Vasko 18, 30tl, FG Trade 9, Naveebird 19t, Sculpies 4-5, Zoff-Photo 23b; **Shutterstock.com:** Paul Brennan 28-29, Dragana Gordic 28b, Red Ivory 6-7

Cover images: *Front:* **Dreamstime.com:** Almoond (Sky), Poemsuk Kinchokawat (Background);
Shutterstock.com: i_mARTy b/ (Grass), Amorn Suriyan b; *Back:* **Dreamstime.com:** Burlesck cra, Cat Vec clb

www.dk.com

A DAY IN THE LIFE OF A
BUILDER

Paige Towler

Contents

6   Meet a Builder
10   On the Job
14   Ready to Work
20   Let's Build!

28 A Job Well Done
30 Glossary
31 Index
32 Quiz

Meet a Builder

Look around you. Are you inside a building? Have you gone over a bridge lately? You have builders to thank.

Builders are people who build things and fix things. They build homes and other buildings. They build roads and bridges. Builders are sometimes called construction workers.

Builders wear long pants. They wear shirts with long sleeves. Heavy boots protect their feet.

Builders work outside. Clothes protect their skin from the sun. If it is cold, clothes keep them warm.

Time to go to work!

On the Job

Building is a big job. A team of builders works together.

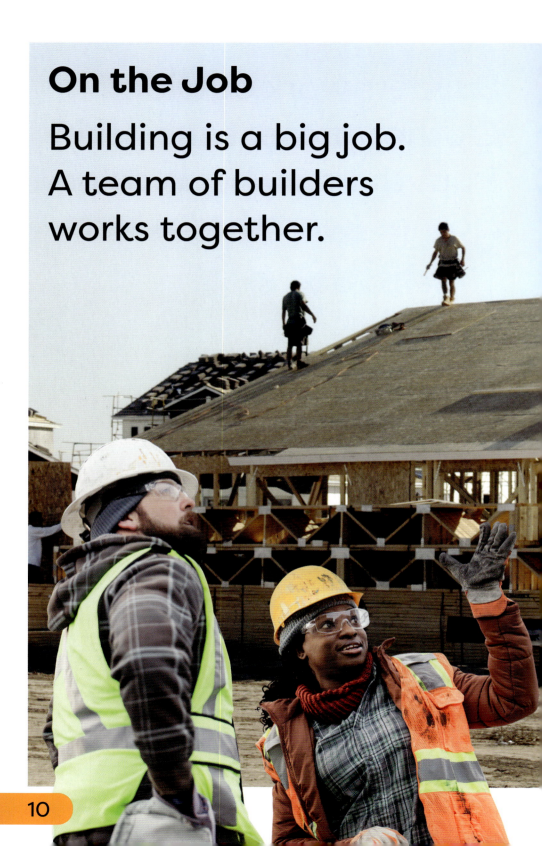

These builders work at a construction site.
This is where they build.

Safety is important. Builders wear special gear to stay safe at the construction site. Thick gloves protect their hands. A bright vest makes a builder easy to see. Goggles keep their eyes safe.

Builders also wear hard hats. These strong helmets protect their heads.

Ready to Work

Builders use different materials to build things. Some builders work with a strong metal called steel. Steel can help hold up tall buildings and bridges.

steel

bricks

wood

These builders are making a house. They will use wood and bricks.

15

First, builders get the site ready. They use tools. Some of these tools are big!

This builder is driving a bulldozer. The bulldozer pushes soil. It flattens the ground.

The builders check their blueprints. A blueprint is a plan for a building. It shows where every part of the building will go.

A measuring tape tells builders how long something is. It helps them make everything the right size.

A builder can also measure space with a laser measure.

Let's Build!

This builder is using a big machine to dig. This machine is called an excavator. The excavator can dig big holes.
The builder digs a hole. The hole will be the basement of the house.

excavator

Another big tool is the crane. Cranes can lift and move heavy things.

Now, the builders make a frame. A frame helps to hold a building up. It keeps the building strong.

crane

frame

Builders use smaller tools, too. They keep these tools in a tool belt.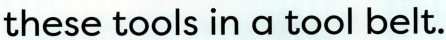

Builders use nails to put pieces of wood together. They hit the nails with a hammer.

This builder is using a drill. A drill is a machine that makes holes. The drill can also push screws into wood. Screws hold pieces of wood together.

The frame is ready!

23

Next, the builders make the walls. This builder is stacking bricks up. A sticky paste called cement holds the bricks together. The builder uses a trowel to make the cement smooth.

trowel

cement

It is time to build the roof! Many roofs are made with shingles. The builders line the shingles up. They use a nail gun to make them stay in place.

nail gun

The roof is ready! The outside of the house is done.

A Job Well Done

It is hard work being a builder! This builder is going home.

She will eat and rest. She will come back tomorrow to build some more.

Glossary

blueprint
a drawing that shows the plan for a building

construction site
a place where many builders work

construction worker
a person who builds roads, bridges, homes, and other buildings

excavator
a big machine that helps dig

laser measure
a small electronic tool used to measure length

Index

blueprints 18

bricks 15, 25

bulldozer 17

cement 25

clothes 8, 9

construction site 11

construction
  workers 7

crane 21

drill 23

excavator 20

frame 21, 23

hard hats 13

laser measure 19

measuring tape 19

nail gun 26

roof 26, 27

safety 12

steel 14, 15

team 10

tools 16, 21, 22

trowel 25

wood 15

Quiz

Answer the questions to see what you have learned. Check your answers with an adult.

1. What are some things a builder wears to stay safe?
2. Name one type of machine you might find on a construction site.
3. What does the frame of a building do?
4. True or False: Builders only use big tools.
5. What holds bricks together?

1. Gloves, boots, vest, ear muffs, goggles, hard hat 2. Bulldozer, excavator, crane 3. It holds the building up 4. False 5. Cement